This book is dedicated to my loving children

Randall, Kenrick, Marcia, and Tyrone. You give me joy, strength and courage to keep going! We have come a long way and share amazing memories. You have been my best friends and buddies.

I love the complicity we share and I cherish you all!

JOURNEYING WITH FAITH

Athina Tsolaki-Franka

CONTENTS

Gratitude

God alone deserves every glory, praise, and honour for this book! The inspiration, the desire and the ability to see it through all came from Him. He placed in my path the right people, at the right time of this journey, and I am grateful for all. I am a mere pencil in the hands of the Author.

My heartfelt gratitude to Fathers Francis Olaseni and Innocent Ezeonyeasi (PHD), for their guidance and counsel on this book writing Journey, and to every other persons who have assisted in anyway in the making process.

Memories of our loved ones and the people we met along the way influence our lives either way, and live indelible traces in us. In every situation, good or bad, there is a lesson to learn. As I often say, no matter the experience, good or bad, keep your chin up as you have learnt something, for life's journey in itself, is a long learning curvy road.

My wish and prayer are that this book will open new dimensions in your life's journey to the Glory of God!

"He is before all things, and in him all things hold together".
Colossians 1:17

PREFACE

This book is a compilation of reflections based on true-life encounters and experiences which aim to fortify, edify and inspire readers to experience a deep, inner-faith encounter in their everyday life journey.

A useful tool in meditations, intentionally written in a free style so to befriend any reader, feel free to appropriate experiences and tap into the prayers. As you journey into this book, I pray that the Lord will meet you in each of the reflections and bless you according to your needs and His desire, for the Bible says in the book of Matthew 6:26: "*And why do you worry about clothes? Look at the flowers in the field. See how they grow. They don't work or make clothes for themselves.*" God cares!

BE BLESSED

—— //// ——

PRIMUS –ANCIENT OF DAYS

The Lord looks at the heart. -1 Samuel 16:7

WHAT MATTERS MOST? Everyone has an outer life and an inner life. The outer life is our public life that everyone can see and that is how we judge others. This is unlike God, who the scripture says in *1 Samuel 16:7*, unlike man, does not look at the outside appearance, but at the heart (inner life).

Now then, have you ever wondered, what the Lord sees when he looks at your heart? The inner life is made up of your thoughts, attitudes, desires, wishes and motives. Only you and God know what is inside. Very often we may go around pretending, acting one way but thinking something entirely different deep within. We may be able to fool people but not God.

God who searches the heart invites us to be open and honest. To go through life transparently. Consider taking an inventory of your thoughts and intentions and ask yourself whether they correspond to your actions? In our weaknesses and

2

imperfection, we aspire to please and serve our God. It is good to remember that even the service, the offerings and blessings we desire to offer him can only be perfected with his perfect touch. Therefore, it is good to submit our ways to the Lord and ask Him to give us an undivided heart so that we can be pleasing to him.

PRAYER

I humbly come before you today, Abba Father, to ask that you search in the deep places of my heart and show me where I need to line up my heart and actions. Help me not to be quick to blame and judge others but to seek to be authentic in my thoughts and actions in Jesus' name. Amen.

OMNIBENEVOLENT GOD

He sends Rain on the Just and Unjust alike. - Mattew 5:45

There is so much happening in the world that we may find overwhelming, to the point we begin to ask ourselves if there is God. No matter how good or comfortable a person might be, one will always come to experience difficulties or storms.

In such a situation, rather than try to use our faith to control our circumstances, it is better to apply faith to adjust the self to withstand the storm and hand over to God. By allowing God to act on your behalf you can remain stable in the storm of life.

Where is God when you suffer? Well, He is right there with you and at work with you deep within. God did not promise that you will not have difficulties whether you are prayerful or not. He promised peace in the storm.

So in times of adversities, do not lose your self-control, pray, stay calm, trust in God as you continue your march in faith and not in emotions. Being at peace is a display of faith in God. Faith reminds us that God is bigger than our problems. God is surely working behind the scenes when we do not seem to notice his presence and soon enough, He will deliver us.

PRAYER

In Your Mercy Father, fill me with your peace, amid the storms of life. I choose to hold on to your peace knowing that you are working behind the scenes. I trust in Your timing, and I know that You will turn everything towards my good in Jesus' name. Amen

YAHWEH TSIDKENU - RIGHTEOUS GOD

*Those who Pursue righteousness and loyalty find life -
Prov 21: 21*

Do you think that righteousness and loyalty go together? Is it possible to be loyal without being righteous? What then is loyalty and who can be called righteous and loyal? Loyal people are honourable people. When you are loyal you stick with someone through thick and thin. When you are loyal, you keep to your word and promises even when there seems to be a 'better' offer. Loyal people respect their leaders, honour their parents, and defend their families. A loyal person builds relationships with integrity, trust, and security. It is however important to remain righteous in other words morally just or correct in pursuing loyalty.

The scripture reminds us that as we pursue loyalty and righteousness, good things will come our way but we are to always remember where we come from, what defines our journey and where we are going. Reflecting on this and remaining truthful to ourselves is very important as it will help us to remain loyal and make us better people. It is noble to consciously strive to be faithful to people around us, keeping promises and mending broken ones, and trying our best to be honest down to the little things honest.

PRAYER

With a Joyful heart, I thank you Heavenly Father, for the promise of life in Your Word. Show me where and how to improve in being loyal. Help me by your Spirit to be more faithful to you and others and to be supportive of those around me. Let your love shine through me as I pursue righteousness and loyalty today, in Jesus' name. Amen

BARACHA – GOD LOVES US

They will receive blessings from the Lord and vindication from God their Saviour Ps 24:5

Are you blessed? What can you do to obtain blessings? And how can you preserve this blessing? This indeed is very deep!

Whilst God wants you to receive every blessing that he has in stock for you, there is a certain order and process to follow and abide by.   The Bible, tells us that it is possible to achieve this, simply by having clean hands and a pure heart. How then can one have a pure and clean heart? The book of John, in 1 John 1:9 says "... *if we confess our sins, He is Faithful and just, to forgive and cleanses us from all unrighteousness"*. The precious blood of Jesus purifies and cleanses us when we turn away from evil acts, go or return wholeheartedly to him, and accept him as our Lord and Saviour. In acknowledging that Jesus died for our sins to redeem us and to set us free, we are accepting that we are cleansed and purified by his blood, and God who is faithful, delivers from bondage and enslavement to ungodly practices.

Reflecting on this passage, I realise that most of the time it is not the big things that keep us from God, but rather very often the small things which we take for granted and hardly pay attention to. These small things may eventually manifest into bigger things firmly rooted which then becomes an obstacle.

You may have watched something on television or the Internet that led to a bad habit that is engrained and pollutes your mind and gradually builds up wrong intentions. It is essential when trapped in such that one seeks the help of God in prayer and a firm desire to make a conscious effort to make a complete change.

It may be difficult but not impossible. It is feasible by making the right choices, and treating others with respect and kindness. If we become a blessing to others, then God's blessings will shower on us as well.

PRAYER

In your infinite Love Lord, help me to be a blessing to everyone I meet. May I turn away from everything that displeases You so to live a righteous life. May the blood of our Crucified Jesus that cleanses and purifies, renews me always. Amen

GIDEON -OMNIPRESENT GOD

We are empowered by our faith in God. Rom 4:20

Past experiences or hurtful situations at times still haunt and torment our thoughts. We begin to wonder if we will ever get over them. If this is you, remember what the Bible tells us in Roman 4:20: "*no unbelief or distrust made him doubt the promise of God but he grew strong and was empowered by faith as he gave praise and glory to God.* This is when you are to put your faith into practice as advised in the book of Hebrew, "*assure yourself and keep on hoping and convincing yourself that it will be over*" (Hebrews 11:1).

God has given us all a measure of faith in order to help us in the difficult moments, so as not to become despondent and to keep on going. However, we need to nurture it. And to nurture it, we need the word of God, we need to listen to or read it as God is the source of our faith and so the more we reflect and pray with the word of God the stronger our faith becomes.

Journeying with Faith

One way to put faith into action is to praise and worship God.

Praise is a supernatural force that causes you to stand strong in faith even when your thoughts or circumstances are coming against the truth. It fills us with peace which in turn keeps our thoughts going in the right direction. Think of reasons to thank God in your life for in thanking him you will praise him and praise make you stable and stronger.

Remember *"I can do all this through him who gives me strength"* (Philippians 4:13). Know and never forget that God gives you inner strength and empowers you to move forward into victory!

PRAYER

With a thankful heart, Heavenly Father, I choose to bless your name. I thank you for my life. I thank you for my breath, for my provision, healing, strength and joy. I praise you and honour Your Name for all your goodness in my life, in Jesus' name. Amen

MERCY - COMPASSIONATE GOD

"For if you forgive other people when they sin against you, your heavenly Father will also forgive your sins, but if you don't forgive others, your Father will not forgive your sins"
- Matthew 6:14-15.

In life, we all have unfair things that happen to us: betrayals, deceptions, rejections, insults, hurts caused by the people we love and trust. In such situation, we only have two options: the first, is to choose to hold on to the hurt or the second, which is to let it go and trust God to heal us.

Remember this: "you don't forgive for their sake; you forgive for your own sake". "When you forgive, you are taking away their power to hurt you. But if you hold on to that offense and stay angry, you are only poisoning your own life and disconnecting yourself from God."

Forgiveness is like a door to your heart. If you shut the door and refuse to forgive, then God cannot forgive you. But when you open the door and allow forgiveness to flow from you, then His forgiveness can flow into you. Choose to forgive and open the door to receive God's life, peace and healing.

PRAYER:

With a thankful heart, my loving Father, I thank You for the gift of forgiveness that sets me free. Help me to truly understand what it means to forgive so I can fully receive Your forgiveness. Give me a humble heart so that I can always ask for forgiveness and forgive my neighbor, in Jesus' name. Amen

EUCHARISTIA - KING OF KINGS

"Now thanks be to God who always leads us in triumph in Christ..." 2 Corinthians 2:14

"He leads us into victory"! In other words, no matter what we face, no matter what is going on in the world around us, no matter what anybody says, we should be thankful to God because victory is on the way and is ours. He is the Almighty and nothing escapes him. He can transform a terrible situation affecting you to your advantage and to the shame of your adversaries. However, we have to be on the path of faith, prayer and good works.

So, knowing he leads us to victory, we don't have to wait for everything to be perfect before we decide to celebrate what God is going to do in our life. That is putting some action behind your faith. In the middle of that adversity or tough time, start making a list of what you will do. That means if you're in the hospital, start planning what you are going to do when you get out. If you lost some money or your bank cards, start planning your coming-out-of-debt party. When things don't look good in the natural, remember, we serve a supernatural God who has the power through the supernatural to change the natural. He will make ways for you always in His own time and way. So stand firm, keep believing and keep on praising him. With God leading you into victory, you can always plan for an increase. You can plan for restoration. You can plan for a comeback that will make you stronger and better than you ever were before!

PRAYER:

I give You thanks and praise my Heavenly Father for the promise of victory. Give me Your vision and Your understanding of it for the future so that I can move confidently into the abundant life You have prepared for me in Jesus' name. Amen.

EMMANUEL - FAITHFUL COMPANION

"Be Strong and Courageous. Do not Fear or be in dread of them, for it is the Lord your God who goes with you. He will not leave you or forsake you" - Deuteronomy 31:6

I serve the God who is always with me no matter what!

God with us... What a gift! When I think of it and when I reflect on the meaning of it, I am filled with joy, I feel reassured and at peace, and a gentle feeling of warmth invades me and travels through me. I feel that no matter the size of the tribulations facing me, I will overcome as He is with me, and if He is with me then nothing can be bigger than me or invincible as He is EMMANUEL, GOD IS WITH US, GOD WITH ME.

The bible tells us that Jesus has many names, all of which identify His character. One of those names is Emmanuel, which means "God with us." Before Jesus came to the earth, the Spirit of God resided in the temple. The people had to go through all sorts of rituals to make them clean enough to go near Him. Now, as believers, we are the temple of the Holy Spirit. The Spirit of the Lord is in him. So when we accept Jesus as our Lord and Saviour, when we dispose our entire self to do his will and obey him he actually makes His home in our hearts – "Emmanuel God with us". He is the one who cleanses us. Isn't it good to know that God is with us? He is closer than the very air we breathe. His peace is always with us. His joy is always with us.

Some time ago I was very sick and got worst in the middle of the night and when I called for an ambulance, there was none. I was in so much pain and despair, then somehow, I remembered that Jesus' name "Emmanuel" means "God with us". And so, I thought to myself, if He is with me, His power is with me. That consoled me, and I began to sing *"Emmanuel, your name is God"* repeatedly. I suddenly felt his peace invade me and overtake me. I was not in panic anymore and was relieved. Isn't that wonderful? To have a God who is always with you. The next time you feel alone, anxious, or in despair, remember, you serve Emmanuel—the God who is always with you no matter what!

PRAYER

With gratitude my Father in heaven, I thank You for choosing to make Your home in me. Thank You for filling me with Your love, peace and joy. I bless You today, knowing that You will never leave me nor forsake me my faithful companion. In Jesus' name. Amen.

BARUCH - GOODNESS

"The Lord bless you and keep you; the Lord make His face shine on you and be gracious to you...and give you peace" - Numbers 6:24-26

Words have tremendous powers in our lives. You can speak life or death, blessing or cursing over your future. However, when you choose to speak the Word of God, you are activating His power in your life. When you speak life and blessing over others, you are blessing them and sowing seed for the harvest in your and their future. God created us in His image and He built everything with his word: *"... He said and let there be light"*(Genesis 1:3). So if He created us in His image, we too carry power in our words.

Be bold to speak a blessing over yourself and your household. Let the blessings sink down deep into your heart and wish the same to your loved ones.

Let us all be a blessing to one another and build a positive and better world centered on the Word and Power of God.

PRAYER

May The Lord bless me and keep me; May the Lord make His face shine on me, be gracious to me and give me peace, in Jesus' name. Amen.

DIES DOMINI

"This is the day the LORD has made. We will rejoice and be glad in it" - Psalm 118:24

Dies Domini finds its literal meaning in an apostolic letter promulgated by Pope John Paul II on July 30, 1998. In this doctrine, Pope John Paul II encouraged the Catholic population to 'rediscover the meaning' behind keeping the Lord's Day Holy. This re-emphasases the 4th Commandment: *"Keep the day of the Lord Holy"* (Deuteronomy 6:21) and how we are to use our time on this day.

The fundamental importance of Sunday has been recognised through two thousand years of history and was emphatically restated by the Second Vatican Council: "Every seven days, the Church celebrates the Easter mystery". This is a tradition going back to the Apostles, taking its origin from the actual day of Christ's Resurrection — a day thus appropriately designated 'the Lord's Day'.

True! Society is evolving and fast changing with new technologies which help us adapt to this ever-changing life. Meanwhile, can technology replace everything? Is attending Mass in person no longer a necessity? Can you receive the Body of Christ wirelessly?

PRAYER

I thank You for my life Heavenly Father! I desire to be close to You and to please You. Take control of my time and give me the disposition to attend Mass, to keep my Sundays Holy as You desire so that in so doing I may glorify Your name through Christ Jesus. Amen.

EL SHADDAI - GREAT GOD

"This is the day that the Lord has made. We will rejoice and be glad in it" - Psalm 118:24

Is Sunday the only important day? Does God desire us to be Glad and Rejoice only on Sunday? Did God not create every other day? I believe that every day is "the day that the Lord has made" and every day that the Lord has made is a special day. Every new day that you wake up to, breathing and kicking is the day the Lord has made for you to rejoice and be glad in it!

I know! Its hard. But guess what: Happiness is not just a random feeling. It is a choice, a decision that one must willfully make by expressing emotion of contentment and satisfaction. Throughout life, we are going to have many challenges of different nature and may go through disappointments that will overtake our mind and preoccupy us so much to the point that it inadvertently deprives us of our joy. It is very easy to let the circumstances of life make us sour and dejected but it will help us to remember that we deserve to be happy, that God created that day for us and so we should receive every new day with joy and gladness.

Make a conscious effort no matter how hard to be happy as you get up in the morning, remembering that if you are alive to witness another new day that the Lord has made it is that the Lord wishes you to rejoice and be glad in it! Offer your day to God and ask Him to fill you with joy. As you choose joy, you are tapping into His strength which will carry you through to victory forever.

PRAYER

With Joy, I thank You my Heavenly King, for giving me another day to bless and serve You. I choose to rejoice today no matter what comes my way. Please give me the mind and body to remember this and let nothing take away Joy and Your peace and strength to overcome in every area of my life, in Jesus' name. Amen.

CONVINCER - TRANSFORMING GOD

"Fight the good fight of the faith. Take hold of the eternal life to which you were called when you made your good confession in the presence of many witnesses"
- 1 Timothy 6:12

When your mind is in agreement with God's Word, it will help guide you toward your destiny. You will have the holy strength and power to see those actions, steps, dreams and desires come to pass in your life! But when you are distracted and concentrated on earthly things, it will be hard to rise and listen to God's directions even though He is there guiding you. It takes daily obedience, prayers, reflections and meditations in our lives.

Sometimes we can get frustrated because we are trying to force things to happen on our timetable, we hold on to things so tightly, and keep on demanding God to make it happen our way without asking ourselves whether this is his will for us, and when it doesn't happen the way we want it, we become even more frustrated and disappointed. Meanwhile, when we finally come to understand that we cannot do it our way, we then drop the stiff-necked attitude as described in the Bible, in Act 7:51, "...*who always resist the Holy Spirit*". It is then that you will realise that you become more willing to let go. If you choose to release that frustration and not to let it become the centre of your attention, and instead, use that same time and energy to be docile to God's will, allowing your steps to be directed by God and open your spiritual door for God to give you the desires of your heart by being docile to His will you will live to see God's plan established in your life.

PRAYER

I submit my mind, desires, thoughts and commitments to you my Heavenly Father, help me to see myself rising higher in every area of my life and bring You glory in everything I do. Use my imagination for Your purpose and guide me in the right direction. Help me to see the dreams You have placed within me coming to pass, in Jesus' name. Amen

THEOPHILUS ~ FRIEND OF GOD

"Keep me as the apple of Your eye..." Psalm 17:8

Why do you think the psalmist expressed the desire to be kept as the apple of God's eye? Do you think he would have made this prayer if he thought that God did not care? Would He who created you and I not care about us? In our day and age, people are important and loved for so many different reasons—titles, position, possessions, power, where you go, what you can do, what you drive etc. But God's value system is very different from the value system of the world. God cherishes and values us so much simply because He made us.

We are the apple of His eye; the centre of His world! He reigns in us!!! If you ever thought that you were not loved, that God had forgotten you, or thought that God has too many other important things on His plate to be concerned with you and your life. Know this today:- God cares and we are his priority. We see this is Jonas 4:10 when he said to Jonas "*I not have concern for the great city of Nineveh, in which there are more than a hundred and twenty thousand people who cannot tell their right hand from their left—and also many animals?* Beloved, *God* values you and your value will never change. You are significant. Your life is significant. The things that concern you, concern God. He carefully watches over every detail of your life, and there is nothing too big or too small for His attention."

God knows every single detail, desire and wishes you have and He takes care of you. So, don't be afraid to take your concerns and cares to the Father. He loves to hear you call upon Him. He is waiting to show Himself strong on your behalf.

PRAYER

With joy, I thank You for loving me, my Father in heaven. Thank You for keeping me as the apple of Your eye. I open my heart and mind to You and cast every care and need on You. As I close my eyes this minute, I receive Your love for me, in Jesus' name. Amen

GIFTED & TALENTED

"A man's mind plans his way, but the Lord directs his steps and makes them sure"   Proverbs 16:9

Everyone has a gift, but not every person recognises what his or her gift is. Being able to identify it is the key to fulfilling the unique purpose of your life. However, don't confuse a gift with talent. Anyone can learn a talent, but a gift is something you are born with.

If you think of your childhood days, you will recall that as a child you had many dreams for the future, dreams of being a captain in the navy, footballer, actress, singer, superhero, president or fireman etc... Meanwhile, most of them have ended up being wishful thinking. As we get older, we grow out of them. It is good to play and have dreams however as we grow older, we must come to know the difference between a God-given dream and a wish or fanciful dream. Beyond our wishes, we all have dreams placed inside of us by the Creator of the universe. Each and everyone has been created for a purpose. One of many ways to tell if a dream is really from God is that you will realise that the desire is not going away. You may have had it for years, but you still can't let it go. At times, realities of life will push you towards it like a coincidence, bringing you very close to it, or imposing it on you in a very weird way.

It is important that we are able to uncover or understand the dream that God has given us. Today, I encourage you to fan aflame the beautiful dream God has planted in you. He placed those desires inside of us for a divine purpose. And as nothing is impossible to Him and since he has desired that dream for you know that He has already paved the way for you to achieve it. All you need to do is to uncover, understand and follow it. Let us help one another to appreciate our God-given personal dreams.

PRAYER

Thank You for the dreams and desires You have placed within me, my Most High God. I submit them to You and ask that You direct my steps. Search my heart and make my thoughts agreeable to Your Word and to Your plan so that I may reach and live every ounce of them, in Jesus' name. Amen

ALPHA AND OMEGA

"We know that in all things God works for the good of those who love Him, who have been called according to His purpose" - Romans 8:28

He is working on your behalf! Isn't it good to know that God is working behind the scenes in your life? No matter what you may be facing, no matter the trials you may be going through, God has a plan to turn things around in your favour. You are called according to His purpose; so right now, He is working out a plan for your good. He is the Master Planner!

He is orchestrating the right people to come across your path. Whatever help or intervention you receive is not a coincidence. He is arranging the right opportunities to open up to you. You may not see it in the natural everyday life but look with your eyes of faith. Come before Him with an open and humble heart trusting that He is guiding you and abandon yourself to His providence. Keep standing. Keep believing. Keep hoping.

Keep declaring His Word and meditate on His goodness, knowing that He rewards the people who seek Him in truth and in spirit.

PRAYER

Heavenly Father, thank You for being the Author, the Alpha and Omega of my life. Thank You for working all things together for my good. Give me Your strength and peace today and fill me with the faith in You which overcomes the world so that I may keep my head up in faith and continue my journey trusting in You alone as my guide, in Jesus' name. Amen.

IMMANENT GOD

"So do not throw away this confident trust in the Lord. Remember the great reward it brings you!" - Hebrews 10:35.

Do you ever look at your life, and ask yourself at times, what is it that God cannot do? Promotion? Healing? Relationships? Freedom from addiction? I do! But I also acknowledge that He has done all that I am and He promised all things in His Word.

God cares. He wants us to live a good life in blessing and wholeness all the days of our life but above all He wants us to trust Him and believe in Him. The bible tells us in the book of Hebrews: *"So do not throw away this confident trust in the Lord. Remember the great reward it brings you!"* (Hebrew 10:35). We must remain faithful and keep on believing and trusting in Him. If we will stay in faith, keep believing, hoping and doing the right thing, God promises there will be a reward. In other words, we should not get discouraged, the reward will surely come.

Journeying with Faith

As we trust Him and stand in faith, as we boldly declare His promises, we are positioning ourselves to receive His blessing. No matter what the circumstances look like, we must remember our payday will come, when we will experience His blessing and reward.

PRAYER

Infinite and Loving Father, thank You for Your good and precious promises, thank you for all the victory and wonders in my life. I desire to trust in You no matter what, and to believe that You are in control and victory is on its way to me. Teach me to understand You, to follow Your commandments and do Your will. Bless me with a *heart that* is fixed on You, in Jesus' name. Amen.

JIREH - MY PROVIDER

"Open your mouth wide, and I will fill it" - Psalm 81:10

Think about birds and many other animals and vegetation in the wild. They have been sustained for generations come and gone by God. Just like birds, God feeds us spiritually when we are receptive to Him.

We need to trust God and abandon ourselves to Him just like birds, who trust to be fed, and say "Feed me O Lord". One way to do this is to always anticipate the goodness of God and keep negative thoughts away. Nurturing negative feelings and thoughts is like closing your mouth. A closed mouth can't be filled. Today Jesus is saying to you and me "open your mouth and let me feed you." Let us hassle and work in faith and trust Him for opportunities beyond our human comprehension.

A baby bird waiting for food is not concerned about where the mother is going to get his food from. He isn't concerned about how she's going to dig it up. No, that bird simply opens its mouth, trusts and waits. Why don't you do the same today? Trust that God is working behind the scenes. Open wide your mouth and let Him feed your life in His way.

PRAYER

In humility, I come to You Lord, asking You to provide for me; I choose to trust You even when I don't understand how everything is going to work out. I know that You are a good God with a good plan for my life. Fill me with Your peace and patience as I humbly wait on You, in Jesus' name. Amen.

PEACEMAKER

"You can simply drop the matter before it turns into something bigger than it needs to" - Prov. 17:14

Too often, we fall into the trap of strife. Someone says something that rubs you the wrong way, and before you know it, there is tension, quarrel, argument and division. The Bible tells us in the Book of James 3:16, that *"strife opens the door to every evil work".* It's the enemy's greatest trap to keep people from a happy and peaceful life. You do not have to fall into this trap, you can rise above it. As the bible verse in Proverb says: *"you can simply drop the matter before it turns into something bigger than it needs to"* (Proverb 17:14). You really do not have to go the way of strife to prove your point.

We are not called to curse the darkness but to light a kindle. If we are going to be all that God called us to be, we have to learn to stay above strife. Instead of letting disagreements pull your relationships apart, look for common ground to draw you closer to the people.

Look for peace and be a blessing. Stay above strife so you can enjoy your relationships and experience God who is Shalom meaning Peace.

PRAYER

With a contrite heart Heavenly Father, I ask forgiveness for the times I picked fight over peace. Today, I choose to stay above strife, and honour You by seeking peace in my relationships. Empower me to walk in love and to be a blessing everywhere I go, in Jesus' name. Amen .

FAITHFULNESS

"Trust in the LORD with all your heart and lean not on your own understanding; in all your ways acknowledge Him, and He will make your paths straight" - Proverbs 3:5-6

We all have times when our plans don't work out. We get delayed, interrupted, and inconvenienced. It's easy to get frustrated and fight against everything that doesn't go your way.

But guess what? Not every interruption is bad. Not every closed door means that you have done something wrong or you are inadequate.

There is such thing as "Divine Interruption" and this is simply when God, on purpose, will delay you, to protect you for a very good reason which you will only understand much later. On purpose, He will close a door because it's not the BEST for you. Sometimes, God will allow us to be inconvenienced so we can help someone else in need. Sometimes, we have to be willing to thread through difficulty so we can be at the right place at the right time. The next time you're interrupted, delayed, or inconvenienced, do not feel regrets rather *get a better perspective and say: "I Trust in YOU LORD with all my heart and believe that you will make my path straight".* Trust in His Divine interruption and Divine intervention.

PRAYER

In simplicity, Heavenly Father, I surrender every area of my mind, will, and emotions to You and chose to TRUST YOU. Use me for Your glory today and teach me to discern Your ways, in Jesus' name. Amen

OMNIPOTENT

"Be anxious for nothing, but in everything by prayer and supplication with thanksgiving let your requests be made known to God" - Philippians 4:6

Do you know that Praise uplifts supplications? When you are praising God it is like putting incense on hot coal just like the psalmist says *"let my prayer rise before you like incense"* *(Psalm* 141:2). Yes I know, you are wondering how can one offer praises when they are hurting? Suffering or anxious?

In fact, that is possible if you will chose to focus on what God can do and not on what is happening to you. God wants us to choose to focus on Him as He is Omnipotent, Omniscient, and Supreme. He is saying to you today that He has your back, He knows your needs, wipe your tears, trust in Him and praise Him for what He is doing for you behind the scene!

Journeying with Faith

What our Lord is saying is that we should not only pray to beg but pray in gratitude. In Divine Mercy, we are offering the sacrifice of God in begging for Mercy and at the same time thanking him for his infinite act of mercy through Jesus for humanity.

PRAYER

With a joyful heart, My God, I thank You and praise You in gratitude for Your love and mercy to me. Bless me with an attitude of grace and enrich my prayers with the help of the Holy Spirit to be filled with an attitude of gratitude always, in Jesus' name.   Amen

SEAT OF WISDOM

"The heart of the wise teaches his mouth, and adds learning to his lips" - Proverbs 16:23

Choosing your words is very important in every conversation. The scripture tells us that in Proverbs 18:21 that *"life and death are in the power of the tongue"*. You can bless your future with your words, or you can curse it. God Himself spoke the world into existence by the creative power of His word.

There are many influences on our words and in the heat of the moment, we often let our emotions dictate what to say. We listen to what others say and allow them to influence our words. We can even be influenced by what we see on television, or the Internet, or read in the news. But a wise person listens to their heart and lets their heart teach them what to say. As a believer, when you listen to your heart, you are tuning in to what the Spirit of God is saying to you. You are coming into agreement with Him.

Journeying with Faith

Listen to your heart. Take time in the presence of the Lord, bring your concerns to Him, be still and quiet before Him. Allow Him to teach you what to do and what to say. As you submit your words and ways to Him, He will direct your path.

PRAYER

I thank You, my God for giving me power in the words of my mouth. Help me to stay tuned into You by listening to You in my heart. Teach me to use my words to always speak life and bless others as Jesus did so as to Glorify You always. Amen.

UNITED IN CHRIST

"So Christ himself gave the apostles, the prophets, the evangelists, the pastors and teachers, to equip his people for works of service, so that the body of Christ may be built up until we all reach unity in the faith and in the knowledge of the Son of God..." - Eph 4;11,13

We need one another in this life. God wants us to work together for His purposes to build the body of Christ in whatever area we work. We all have a part to play. St Paul puts it creatively and says: *"... some plant seeds, some water, and some bring in the harvest"* (1 Corrinthians 3:6-8). No matter the role we have, when we work together, we are honouring God. It pleases Him when we partner with one another to put in practice the good news of the Gospel.

In Romans 10;14 it is said: *"And how can they believe in him if they have never heard about him"*? That is where we all come in, whether is words, actions or behavior God wants us to work together with and for one another, and in so doing we will show Him to others. God wants us to be the link of the Gospel. Our discussions and behaviour need to be able to tell others about Jesus who paid the price of our salvation.

What's your part? What's mine? We are all important parts of the body of Christ. Whether you minister in the pulpit or on the street corner, whether you sow seed so that others can nurture, whether you motivate with a simple pat on the back or give a supportive smile to someone who needs it, we are all important. Never underestimate the part you can play because together we are building his kingdom and in did a better world.

PRAYER

Thank You Almighty Father, for giving me a part to play in building Your Kingdom. I dedicate back to You the resources You have given me. Use me for Your glory, by the Power of the Holy Spirit, in Jesus' name. Amen.

MY DELIVERER

"You keep track of all my sorrows. You have collected all my tears..." - Psalm 56:8

Does God record sorrows and collect our tears?

He cares about our thoughts, feelings, and emotions. He knows everything that we go through: joy, tears, passion, pains and sorrows, project, success, failures, ambitions etc.... In fact we are so important to Him that He records every sorrow and collects every tears we shed. He is aware of every wrong that has ever been done to you so that He can make up for every single one of them.

He is working to bring restoration and peace to you. The One who collects your tears will restore every broken plan into your life. He is our Strength and Vindicator. He cares so much about every detail of our life that He wants to restore everything that has ever been stolen. He wants to heal every single hurt and pain. He sees the longings and desires of your heart.

My dear, know that He is working things out for your good! Keep standing, keep believing, and keep doing the right thing because Your God is your Strength and Vindicator. So now wipe your tears and pray.

PRAYER

In your infinite Goodness, Abba Father, I thank You for loving me and setting me free. Thank You for being my Vindicator. I choose to release every hurt, pain and sorrow, knowing that You will make all things new for me in Your time, in Jesus' name. Amen.

GRACIAS

"But I, with a song of thanksgiving, will offer sacrifice to you. What I have vowed I will make good. Salvation comes from the LORD" - Jonah 2:9

When we are worried we run to God asking for solution or victory and when happy we sing, we dance we praise Him. However when things don't go the way we want, we often moan, complain and forget to say "Thank You." We forget or choose not to praise Him and that is the wrong attitude.

I have grown to understand that God is supreme in every area. He holds the reigns and knows things before they happen and already knows the outcome too. He says, in the book of Jeremiah: *"I the Lord, search the heart and examine the mind, to reward each person according to their conduct, according to what their deeds deserve"* (Jeremiah 17:10). God seems to say to us, do not look at what you think is not right but look at what I have done for you, and let Me take care of the rest. Whilst in the fish, Jonah suffered the trauma and anxiety, however he understood that God is supreme, only Him can set him free and that it is not through a rebellious attitude that he will make it but by humility. Jonah praised God and at once God ordained the fish to vomit him. Like Jonah, we too can be stubborn, and need to remember that God is supreme. His love towards us will never end as he gently brings us to the understanding of His will and way. God always moulds us with gentle love and care.

PRAYER

In Your Infinite Goodness, oh Lord, bless me with the right attitude and disposition at all times and keep my eyes focused on all You have done so that I will forever praise You, in Jesus' name. Amen

MIGHTY

"For whatsoever is born of God overcometh the world"

- 1 John 5:4

Guess what? It doesn't matter that things get bad all around you, that people are negative, complaining and discouraged. Don't let that spirit rub off on you and bring you to that level. As CHILDREN of GOD, we are called to SHINE and EXCEL!!! Notice the scripture says *"For whatsoever is born of God overcometh the world"* (1 John 5:4), so the worse it gets in the world the brighter it's going to be for God's people as we are called to SHINE and EXCEL!!

Now then, what are your ambitions? your plans? What would you like to achieve in your life? Have you thought of it? Have you reflected on your life? Have you entrusted your project to the Lord? Or are you seating down worrying, fearing the future, asking the how and what and when you will achieve your dream? Thinking that is not really for you...??? Remember: It doesn't matter that people are negative, complaining, and discouraged, the darker it gets in the world the brighter it's going to be for God's people as *"whatsoever is born of God overcomes the world"* (1 John 5:4).

It is up to you to believe, get up and claim success over your future. As you do, you'll enlarge your vision and make room for God to do amazing things in every area of your life! TRUST in HIM and CAST your BURDEN on HIM!

PRAYER:

I thank you, Heavenly Father, for Your promise and I entrust into Your care my ..... (name your project or desire), it does not matter that it is gets darker around me as I know that its getting brighter for me. Thank you for working behind the scene for my success, in Jesus' name. Amen!

ALMIGHTY - ALL-SUFFICIENT ONE!

"... the Lord appeared to Abram and said to him, 'I am Almighty God" - Genesis 17:1

The original Hebrew word in the verse above is "El Shaddai" and it means "the All-Sufficient One" or "the God of plenty". Yes, not me, but He says it, He is more than ENOUGH. Our God is more than COMPLETE!

He does not worry about how He is going to meet your needs as He has it ALL. He does not wonder about how He's going to provide for you as He is already overflowing with everything you need in this life, and He longs to bless you.

All He wants you to do is to trust in Him, to bring Him your burdens and believe in Him. He wants to bless you abundantly so that you can turn around and be a blessing to other people, not only in the material aspect but spiritually, physically and mentally too. He wants you to be His reflection on the earth. For that, you have to first receive what He wants to do in your life. nYou can't go around with a negative, self-defeating attitude and expect to see the blessings of God pour in. No, the Bible tells us that it is our faith that pleases God: *"It will be given to you according to your faith" (Matthew 9:29).*

So keep an attitude of faith and expectancy at all times knowing that you serve the Almighty God who promises to supply all your needs because He is "El Shaddai", the more than complete God, the Alpha and the Omega, the Most High and Most Powerful One!!!

PRAYER:

In Jesus Mighty Name, I believe that You can supply all my needs. You are the God of more than enough. Today, I receive Your Word in my life and choose to have an attitude of faith and expectancy. Thank You for Your goodness and faithfulness to me. Amen.

FAITH

"Faith comes by hearing, and hearing by the Word of God"
- Romans 10:17

As per the above title, the Bible tells us that faith comes by hearing the word of God. It does not say that faith comes when you have heard but says "by hearing..." this means that it is a continued process. The more you hear the word of God the closer to him you get, and the more your faith in Him increases! Notice, all In the present tense!!!

No doubt, the word of God can transform instantly; but we need to hear God's principles over and over again so that they become engraved and active in our lives. God's truth sets us free and puts His plan for our lives into motion. As you hear and study the word of God, it chisels away the doubt and unbelief that has build up over the years.

Just as a seed needs water to grow daily, our spirit needs the word of God everyday. We need Him in our lives, and if we will make room for Him, He will be there everyday to nourish, strengthen and walk with us everyday! The more you hear God's word, the more you know Him, understand His principles, promises and believe His word.

"I already do it" I hear you say! Yet, at times you slip. The truth is that the more you invest yourself in His word the closer you get to Him.

So why not abandon yourself to Him and ask Him to draw you nearer to Him? to give you the wisdom to look for His word, read, understand and make it a living part of your life? The more you hear the word of God, the more your faith will grow moving you forward and freely into your victory!

PRAYER:

Your word Most High God, is alive, active and growing in my life. I submit myself to You today and I thank you and ask that you teach me Your ways and give me the intelligence and wisdom to read and look for Your word so that I may know You better and live a better life, in Jesus' name. Amen.

EMPOWERED

*"Because every child of God is able to defeat the world.
And win the victory over the world by means of our faith"*
- I John 5:4

Every single one of us is exposed to challenges now and again, and it is perfectly natural as we live in this world full of surprises and are mere mortals. However, as children of God, we should have a different way to respond to those challenges. Yes, *"many are the trials of the just but the Lord sees them through"* (Psalm 34:19). We all have things that come against us, but God didn't create us to be overwhelmed and overcomed. He created us to be overcomers! Winners and Triumphant!!!

What is your situation today? Are you facing some challenges or experiencing some unexpected setbacks? What is your attitude? Where is your faith? *"It will be given to you according to your faith!!"* (Matthew 9:29). Remember?? Think about it for a minute. When something isn't going your way time after time... what do you do? Sit back and give up? It may well be easy to get down and discouraged, feeling sorry for yourself, but know that if you go around thinking it's never going to work out, your attitude is limiting what God can do. But if you keep your chin up, dig your heels firmly in faith with assertiveness knowing that God is bigger than your problems and that He already has a way out, fight a good fight of faith, and continue to work for your solution, then you are ALLOWING God to manifest and turn whatever negative situation around!!!

REMEMBER: you are created to OVERCOME, WIN AND CONQUER! Stand strong with the attitude of an OVERCOMER and watch what God will DO on your behalf!

PRAYER:

Thank You for making me an overcomer in Jesus' name. You are El-Shaddai, the God that is more than ENOUGH and NOTHING if IMPOSSIBLE to YOU, I trust that You are bigger than my problems and that You are working on my behalf. Thank You for the victory that You have in store for my future! In Jesus' name. Amen.

NISSI - THE LORD, MY STRENGTH

"No weapon formed against you shall prosper..."

- Isaiah 54:17.

What does it really mean?? We say it, confess and proclaim it. Do we really understand what it means? The truth is that if you choose to believe in Christ as Lord and Saviour, if you honour God and trust in Him and do His will, you benefit from certain invisible grace. God blesses you with protection, favour and mercy that surround you like a shield. He puts a blood line around you that the enemy cannot and will never cross, and that is the blood of Jesus, as believers of *Jesus "we are covered by the blood of Jesus"!!!!* (1 John 1:7). No matter the situation, or problem, no matter the duration, in the end it is not going to PROSPER!!! God is going to turn the situation to your advantage and you will overcome it!!!

That is the heritage that God gives to those who are His, those who give Him the first place in their lives.

Important! God has not said that we will never have problems... No, life itself is full of difficulties, the promise God is making to us is that when things go against us, since we have kept our covenant with Him, we will overcome the problem and it will never prosper, He will turn it to our advantage!!!

So, what is your situation at present time? Are you going through difficulties? Your marriage? Your finances? Your job or education? Your inner peace, health or life in general? Call on God and remind Him that He said in the book of *Isaiah, that « no weapon fashioned against you shall prosper »! (Isaiah 54:17).*

PRAYER:

My LORD and GOD, thank You for the promises that I found in Your word. I choose today to accept Your word is the truth that will set me free. I declare by faith that no weapon formed against me shall prosper, in Jesus' name. Amen.

CARITAS - LOVE ONE ANOTHER

"To give to the poor is like Lending to the Lord, and the Lord will pay you back" - Pov.19:17

Isn't our God wonderful? Gold and silver belong to Him. He is the one that gives us and blesses us with all that we have. Meanwhile, He tells us that when we give to the poor we are actually LENDING to Him and that He will PAY us BACK!!! Who else do you know is capable of that? The reality is that God wants us to use our own initiative to be a blessing for others and ourselves, whether materially by giving to others or spiritually by praying for others, sharing or preaching the Gospel.

Often people are tempted to think that they only have little or not enough for themselves and so difficult to give, or that it is not worth giving as what they would give would only be little, but don't forget that the little you are thinking to give might be but a lot to your neighbour.

Also, you don't always need to have a lot to be a blessing to someone else. Remember: *"I was hungry and you fed me, I lacked clothes and you clothed me, I was thirsty and you gave me drink...!"* - Matthew 25:42 and *"Faith without charity is a dead faith"* (James 2:17). So let's not sit back but continue to be a blessing in any way that we can and give to the needy.

PRAYER:

I praise Your mighty name, My Lord and God, and thank You for all Your blessings in my life. Please make me a source of blessing for others and teach me to recognise the various ways that I can bring help to the needy. In Jesus' name. Amen!

GOODNESS

"If you are willing and obedient, you will eat the best from the land"
- Isaiah 1:19

God wants us to have "HIS VERY BEST"; He doesn't want us to just barely get by in life. He wants us to thrive and overflow with His goodness. But for that He requires us to have the right attitude — We have to be willing and obedient. It's not just doing what the word of God says but about having the right attitude.

It is one thing to give as the Bible says in Hebrew 13:16 – *"Do not neglect to do good and to share what you have..."* and it is another thing to help because you understand that you will be a blessing to another.

It is one thing not to judge because the Bible says not to and it is another thing not to judge because you realise and understand that we all make mistakes, and so you want to forgive, and want help your neighbour. That is being obedient and willing. That is having an overflow of mentality. That is to understand what God wants us to do so we can be a blessing to others. And if we can be willing and obedient, we will see that there is no limit to what God will do in our life!

Today, make the decision to be willing and obedient and watch His blessings overflow in every area of your life.

PRAYER:

In Your Mercy, Heavenly Father. Help me to find ways to be a blessing to others as You pour out increase in every area of my life in this special week and all times to come, so to honour You in all that I do, in Jesus' name. Amen.

DIVINE MERCY

"...In this world you will have trouble. But take heart! I have overcome the world" - John 16:33

Every now and then, situations come against us. They try to steal our joy and rob us of the victory, peace and joy that God has put in us. Hurts, words, behaviours, actions, matters, name it... often even from the people we would least expect and those we trust...

In fact, do you know that throughout your whole life, the enemy has one mission? That is to kill, steal and destroy your joy, hope, vision and happiness? and so, he works and works on anything and anyone that would lead him to you? I love what the above verse says and that is the KEY to the understanding I need you to have!

Now LISTEN: It starts by warning us *"In this world you will have trouble"* then it reassures us *"take heart"* meaning "Be of good cheer" "Don't Panic" or "Relax"!!! Then it ends with *"I have overcome the world!"* YES HE HAS!!! God knows that we will have trouble. He knows that we will hear, see or experience things that will hurt, demoralise or even destroy us that is why He immediately reassures us, right after saying *"in this world you will have trouble,"* and not only He reassures but He actually reminds us that He has overcome the world!

So with this, realise and understand that you are overcomer in Christ Jesus and be joyful no matter what the circumstances or situations and don't allow emotions take the best part of you!

Therefore, stop struggling on your own and turn to Him and tell Him: "Lord you have overcome the world for me, let me experience the Joy of it"! Jesus lived a human life like us even though He did not do all the things we do, he can understand human nature, pain and hurt. He is the one that changes situation and people. So when life is difficult, disappointing and painful, in your own way and own words tell Him how you feel and let him turn things around in his way and time. REMEMBER: We are overcomers through Christ Jesus!

PRAYER

I humbly come to You today ABBA Father and entrust to you my hurt, pain and disappointment. In Your LOVE Turn them into Joy and help me stay focused on eternal things. I choose to have joy and peace no matter what comes my way because I know I have the ultimate victory in You, in Jesus name. Amen.

YESHUA - SON OF GOD

"...For I am Gentle and Humble of Heart" - Mathew 11:29

I watched a film yesterday which really got me thinking! A couple, husband and wife were ready to sacrifice their daughter through rituals in exchange of money... And they DID!!! Though this was a movie, I hear movies are often made from real issues... This couple wanted wealth, power, influence and life to the point selfishness overtook the centre of their hearts. They refused their daughter the right to live, this miracle called "breath of Life" from GOD that meets us every day when we wake up in the morning! Her life was taken away for personal interests and she was refused the right to life!

On the contrary, we have JESUS who is the GREATEST amongst all, yet made himself SERVANT of all! Everyone aspires to be like Jesus! How far can we go?

Journeying with Faith

Everyone has aspirations. You want to be great, honoured, respected and powerful, but who is really at the service of others? Who really is ready to give his life for another? How often do you volunteer to do things or help others? How often do you step back and allow others to take lead? How often do you put aside your precious personal interest so as to allow others to breathe? A Great Soul generates Great Love and a Heart Full of Grace!

PRAYER:

Jesus meek and humble of heart make my heart like into yours; grant me the Grace to Desire to be like You always. Amen.

ELOHIM - GOD IS JUST

"From all their distress the Lord rescues the just" - Ps 34:4

I used to cry, moan and complain to God: "Why do I have to go through this Lord? Why does it have to be me? Why am I treated this way?" This sounds familiar right? Is this not what most of us do, assuming that as we pray and believe in God we must never have issues? Then, once all is fine, we quickly forget!

There are times when I recall certain struggles and wonder how I had possibly overcomed... How is it that despite all difficulties and against every odd I was successful...? Well beloved, that is because He came to my rescue, He set me free; He gave me the strength and mind to overcome, and opened the right door with the right people for me!!! He is the solution... He never said that we will not endure difficulties but that He will rescue us from ALL our DISTRESS!!!

So when you feel afflicted, when distressed do not cry like I used to "why me... why me..." but instead bring your tears to the Lord, present Him your affliction and distress and let Him come to your rescue. He will give you the strength, mind and support needed. But remember, His ways are not our ways.

Whatever it is, financial difficulties, and personal or health issues nothing is too big for Him, talk to Him and watch Him come to your rescue.

PRAYER?

With a thankful heart, I thank you for Your promise Heavenly Father. I offer You (name you problem) and ask that You help me not to worry anymore. Grant me the faith to always look on to You no matter what, in Jesus' name. Amen.

AGAPE

"Carry Each other's Burdens and so you will fulfil the Law of Christ" - Galatians 6:2

One cannot work on their own... We need the help of one another. It's amazing how God can take so many people in the world and set up a plan for them all. One cannot work on their own... We need the help of one another. God wants us to work together for His purpose to build the body of Christ. We all have a part to play. The Bible says, in 1 Corinthians 3:9 *"For we are God's Fellow workers. You are God's field, God's building".* No matter what role we have, when we work together, we are honouring God. It pleases Him when we partner with others.

With this in mind, ask yourself: How often do you team up with others? Tolerate and share your thoughts or work with other one another? How often do you step in to help? Or rescue others?

PRAYER

I humbly come to You today, Father God, to thank You for giving me a part to play in building Your Kingdom. I dedicate back to You the resources You have given me. Use me for Your glory, in Jesus' name. Amen.

MY HIDING PLACE

"In the day of trouble he will keep me safe in his dwelling"
- Psalm 27:5.

Sometime ago, I dreamt over some consecutive nights, that I was being chased and that I was running to hide in a church... Reflecting on the meaning of this as I write this book, I have a flashback of me playing "hide and seek" with my little "TATEE" who tiptoeing in the house or in the garden will find the best hiding place to hide and wait quietly for me to find him! Children love this game. Although as a game, at times they hide as a means of protection or to escape a situation i.e. not to be called to help with a task or chores.

The truth is that even adults, need a good place to hide from time to time. Sometime we need a place of refuge, a place of safety, a place to rest when feeling overwhelmed, a place where the enemy of our soul can never find us.

Journeying with Faith

The Psalmist says *"In the day of trouble he will keep me safe in his dwelling"* (Psalm 27:5).

Why was I, in my dream, running in a Church? The Church is the place of worship and prayer where the Eucharist is, where Jesus is present and where we invoke God's mercy.

God is the perfect hiding place for us! He promises to hide you and me! He is the Fortress, the Shelter and Strength!

There's only one true place of safety and rest for your soul, and that is in the arms of Jesus. Know that He loves you, and He is ready to receive you when you call His name! *"Come to me and I will give you rest"* (Matthew 11:28-29).

Where do you pray? Who do you run to? Where is your hiding place?

PRAYER

I humbly come today, before You, Heavenly Father, giving You all that I am and offer you my loved one. Thank You for hiding me and the person reading this prayer in Your shelter and keeping us safe from the storms of life, in Jesus' name. Amen.

MY PERFECTER

"Whatever you do, work at it with all your heart, as working for the Lord, not for men" - Colossians 3:23

God doesn't bless mediocrity! He blesses excellence!

Ways of life often weigh us down and gradually cause negligence, low or poor performance.

For example, today's society with challenges derived from COVID related issues can be overwhelming and there is a tendency to accept or tend to accept the minimum and make it the norm... the "do as little as you can to get by" and then look for the easy way out... We tend to forget that whatever we do, we should do it to the best of our ability, set the standard and remember that we are ultimately working for the Lord.

Doesn't the Bible tell us: *"Whatever you do, work at it with all your heart, as working for the Lord, not for men"? (Colossians 3:23).*

Journeying with Faith

He's the one who put those talents and abilities in you and me, he knows what we can or cannot do and so ask that we do it to the best of our abilities. We are a steward of the gifts he's given us... We are children of the Almighty, Excellent God, called to excellence. We bring him glory in all we do and so we should offer Him all we do so He can perfect all to His standard. Whatever you do, work at it with all your heart, as you are working for the Lord, not for men"...

PRAYER

With confidence, Almighty God, I choose today a path of excellence. I offer You all that I am and do. Keep me close to You by the power of the Holy Spirit and help me to rise up higher in every area of my life, in Jesus' name. Amen.

WAY MAKER

"... You love him, you believe in Him and are filled with an inexpressible and glorious joy" - 1 Peter 1:8

We all experience things or situations that affect our joy and enthusiasm... We feel weak, anxious, worried about the 'what will it be' or 'what would be said or thought' etc... Not wrong! It's a natural reaction. However as children of the Most High, as His 'Chosen ones' as you are given a particular mission.... You need to remember that you were created, born for a purpose, we can read about this in the Bible in various books' however, Proverb 16:4. *"The Lord created everything for its purpose".* God has you here on purpose for a purpose. And since you are one of His Chosen ones sent here for a purpose know that He has your back. And if He who sent you for a purpose has your back why then be sad, panic and worry? Is He not the Glorious, Joyous, Almighty GOD?

Listen, it's time to get excited about your future and learn to enjoy each and every day again and again. Get your Joy Back!

You see, if you don't make the conscious effort to keep your joy, not only will the enemy rob you of the joy that belongs to you, but he'll rob your family and friends of the gift that you have to give them... When you have joy, you can use that joy to influence the people around you for good. Joy is strength and so you can offer strength to the people God has placed in your life that you meet every day, even if it is by exchanging a smile! Make a conscious effort to let Joy flow from within, keep your heart open and let your faith in Him fill you with inexpressible and glorious joy!

PRAYER

In Your Infinite Goodness, Heavenly Father, receive my prayer as I thank You for Your love. Thank You for choosing me and moulding me into Your image. Please fill me with Your inexpressible, glorious joy so that I can be a blessing to the people You have placed in my life, in Jesus' name. Amen.

MIGHTY WARRIOR

"The Lord will fight for you, and you shall hold your peace and remain at rest" - Exodus 14:14

Life experience taught me that no matter what we do, we will always have critics. There will always be difficult people around who for one reason or another will try to upset us, steal our peace and joy. Listen, you don't have to let them succeed. You can decide to take the high road and let God fight that battle!

There are people who no matter what you say or do will not accept you. They will always come up with unfair judgement, provocation, they simply don't want to be at peace and want to trouble your peace.

When Jesus sent out His disciples to certain homes, the Bible tells us in the book of Luke, that he said: *"speak peace over those homes, and if they don't receive the peace that you're offering, it will come back to you..."* (Luke 10:6-7). In other words, if you do your best to be at peace with people but still they won't take your peace that PEACE will just come back to you in double portion! You'll not only get your peace, but you'll get their share as well! God sees and rewards.

PRAYER

In Your infinite Goodness, Peace-giving Father, please fill me with Your peace and help me hold my peace and share it even when the wrong attitude is affecting me. I trust that You are fighting my battles for me, in Jesus' name. Amen.

JESUS

"I am the vine. You are the branches. If you abide in me, you will bear much fruit and your fruit will remain" - *John 15:5*

The cycle of life walks us into numerous situations, challenges, tests, trials at times more difficult than others. We face trials and temptations where a person's character is being developed and faith in God is being strengthened. Sometimes challenges can be so rigid that it feels like you are not progressing, at times even as if you are regressing instead of stagnating. On other occasions it is as if you are progressing so fast that you begin to doubt whether you are on the right path... If one is not careful, he'll start swimming in doubt, confusion and even when things are going well he'll start looking for things to go wrong...

True, we all have ups and downs. However God doesn't want us to be living life like a roller coaster... He wants to bring us to a place of stability where we remain strong in Him. Jesus said: *"I am the vine. You are the branches. If you abide in me, you will bear much fruit and your fruit will remain" (John 15:).* The word "remain" means "to be fixed, immovable, not affected by circumstances." If you will just keep abiding in Him, just keep meditating on His Word, He'll bring you through. He'll make you strong, He'll keep you stable, and you'll keep moving forward into the life of blessing He has prepared for you! It doesn't mean that all will be Kings and queen but it means that whatever type of life, in whatever role you find yourself in you will live with joy and confidence...

PRAYER

In your love, hear me Yahweh, as I set my heart and mind on You knowing that You are good and faithful. Help me trust that as I seek You and put You first, You will direct my steps. Help remains firmly rooted in You knowing You are leading me, in Jesus' name. Amen.

GRACE WITH GRATITUDE

"Praises Go Up and Blessings Come Down" - Psalm 133

No matter what is going on in life, we can find a reason to thank God. Do you know that what you dwell on is what you will draw into your life? You can either focus on your problems, or you can focus on your blessings. The choice is Yours!

One thing I've noticed is that when I live with an attitude of gratitude, not only I see every positive thing that is happening to me for which I thank God, but I even start thank Him for what He is doing behind the scene without me knowing.

I get excited about the future. We have many reasons to thank Him: Being alive, having a roof, good health, perhaps not perfect but coping, have the Right People around us etc...

Journeying with Faith

When you say "thank you" to God for the things that are coming, it's really a declaration of your faith in Him. I strongly believe that this is the kind of faith that pleases God. In fact, the Bible says: *"Rejoice always, pray without ceasing, give thanks in all circumstances for this is the will of God"* (Psalm 107:1).

When we trust in His goodness and believe that He is a destiny-changing God for those who diligently seek Him.

PRAYER

Dear father of all Mankind, please help me see Your hand of blessing at all times even in little things. As I continually acknowledge and praise You, continue to bless me, in Jesus' name. Amen.

POWER IN WORDS

"It has the Power of Life and Death" - Proverb 18:21

I have always believed that if the Spirit of God is in us, since God created the world with words He spoke, then we too have the tremendous creative power with the words that we speak and can confess positive and claim victory in our days, project and life.

If we can apply this to our daily life and keep a positive attitude, an attitude of faith then we will see glory and victory in our lives.

Today, I woke up very tired, I had little sleep and have not been in the best of me lately, my day could have easily been ruined however, I thought to myself as I got up: God gave us the power in the tongue, trouble is inevitable (I didn't choose not to sleep) but misery is optional (up to me to be happy or miserable...)! I then chose to claim a successful day and claimed my joy, I confessed that my day was going to be of an achiever, that I will hold on firm and excel in whatever I was going to do... Guess what? It was a BRILLIANT DAY! And if it worked for me? why won't it work for you? Choose to speak life over your future, choose to speak success, peace and victory. Have a vision of an achiever and winner no matter what and work towards your goal.

Stop confessing negativity: I am weak, this is all I can do, I can't handle this, I can't do it, it's always like that, am not the best...

PRAYER

I thank you Father Almighty for giving me tremendous power in the word of my mouth, teach me to confess positively, to claim my victory and to glorify you in all I do, in Jesus' name. Amen.

ABRAHAM'S BLESSINGS

"The Lord bless you and keep you; the Lord make His face shine on you and be gracious to you...and give you peace" - *Numbers 6:24-26*

As I worshiped my God this morning and entrusted my day to Him, I confessed THESE words from the book of Numbers 6:24-26 over my life and that of my family. I said: " *The Lord bless us and keep us; the Lord make His face shine on us, be gracious to us and give you peace".*

I remembered the power of WORDS and knowing that God's Words are powerful, I chose to speak the word of God over myself and family. The truth is, when you do this, you are activating His power in your life. When you speak life and blessing over others, you are blessing them and sowing seed for the harvest in yours and their future. Words have tremendous powers in our lives. Remember: God built everything with His words: "...and let there be light".

So speak positively of yourself, profess and proclaim good words and be a blessing to others.

PRAYER

Oh God in Your infinite goodness, bless me, my family and loved ones, and keep us Yours. In Your love, make Your face shine on us, be gracious to us and give us your peace, in Jesus' name. Amen.

CONVENANT KEEPING

"...If you Obey Me Fully and Keep my Covenant then out of ALL Nations You will be my chosen one..." - Exodus 19:5

On reflecting on the above scriptures, why do you think God is striking a deal with his children, even though all are His?

The Book of Isaiah in the Bible tells us that God "*created us without our permission and for His own Glory*"! (Isaiah 43:7)

God does not restrain us. He loves us, He has taught us what is good and bad in His sight and wants us to freely decide to obey Him. And this is why I believe He made this covenant. Almost like parents reward their children i.e. if you will be obedient, I will give you this, or do that, or again see to this.

Then, knowing that He is able to do all things, why would we not opt to side with Him? Choose to do His WILL and LEARN to UNDERSTAND His WAYS through Prayers and Meditations and TRUST that God is working for our good?

Why not BELIEVE that He FEEDS our spiritual self and is

always ready to do so but needs us to COOPERATE with Him?

Today, tell Him you are ready to do HIS WILL and look up to HIM to guide you, let Him do His part and you do yours.

PRAYER:

I humbly ask you, All Powerful and Covenant Keeping God, to show me Your Ways. I chose to trust You even when I don't understand how everything is going to work out as I know that You never fail anyone, in Jesus' name. Amen

OMNIFICENT

"Give generously to them and do so without a grudging heart; then because of this the Lord your God will bless you in all your work and in everything you put your hand to"
- Deuteronomy 15:10.

Does giving and sharing not remind you of Christmas? What is Christmas? Is it not about giving, sharing? The expression of "the Word made flesh"? The gift that God gave us all in the birth of His son who was destined to die so to give humanity salvation?

At Christmas, we exchange gifts and share things out of love for one another... then again, can one not give without loving? i.e. out of respect? So yes, people can give without loving, but no one can love without giving... Love prompts us to give of ourselves, our time, abilities and resources even at times what we don't have. The Bible tells us that *"God is love, and the world will know we are His followers by our love — and our giving shows our love" (John 13:35).* Have you ever thought of how your love affects your giving? God is love and He gave us all He is himself "Love" in the birth of his son so that whoever believes in him does not perish but receives eternal life...

So when Christmas comes, let us remember to take time to focus on the greatest gift of all, the gift of Eternal and Abundant life through Jesus "Emmanuel, God with *us*".

PRAYER

In Your Divine Power, come to me, Emmanuel God with us, and those who are yet to unwrap you in them, to those who don't understand the value of your coming and love, and to those who consistently reject you so all may have You for Eternity. Amen

MERCY

"For if you forgive other people when they sin against you, your heavenly Father will also forgive you. But if you do not forgive others their sins, your Father will not forgive your sins" - Matthew 6:14-15

Some years ago, when I was a Catechist, preparing children for the Holy Communion Sacrament, I reflected with them on "the Gift of Forgiveness". I felt very drawn by this topic and still do. That is certainly because it is a key element of our spiritual growth...

In life, we all have unfair things that happen to us; betrayals, deceptions, rejections, insults, hurts by the people we love and trust most, at times we upset ourselves more than necessary by misunderstanding the situation. We then feel so hurt and sad. That said, we only have 2 options... We can choose to hold on to the hurt, become bitter and angry, and let it poison our future; or, we can choose to let go of it and trust God to make it up to us. However, it is not always easy! We often feel we struggle to forgive because the hurt is so bad and unknowingly, we become defensive or resist forgiveness, giving reasons and arguments and recounting how painful or hurt we felt. Remember, God is Mercy. And if He is Mercy, He can help us achieve this if we will turn to Him asking Him to help us to forgive as we offer Him the hurt or issue of concern.

Jesus taught one prayer which is also the praying model. We commonly call it "the Lord's Prayer; part of it is about forgiveness, it says: *"forgive us as we forgive those who trespass against us"* (Matthew 6:9-13). In other words we are to be forgiven in the same way and protion that we forgive others!

PRAYER

In Your Fountain of Love, Heavenly Father, I offer every hurt and sorrow. I offer my disposition and love. Help me to forgive and let go of every hurt, trusting that You are restoring and vindicating me, in Jesus' Name. Amen.

FATHER OF LIGHTS

"Thy Word is a lamp unto my feet, and a light unto my path" - Psalm 119:105

This Bible passage quoted above is the reason we have a Bible, the reason we need to read it, the reason we need to meditate on what it says, what it advises and should choose to live according to it.

We are here on earth for a period of time. Some longer than others, and at the end of our days, we are to return to our creator, who created us for a purpose, and I would like to believe that we do want to be able to say, when that time comes: *"I have fought the good fight, I have finished the race, I have kept my Faith"!* (2 Timothy 4:7). Meanwhile, to achieve this, we need a reminder, a guide to help us understand how we are to run this race (our life here on earth) and prompt us on the things we can do, those we should not do, and how to go about or make amends when we mess up.

Journeying with Faith

The Bible puts together the Word of God, the teaching of Jesus, his disciples' experiences as well as those of inspired proclaimers of the Will of God, to help teach us how to obey the Word of God so as to live confidently and freely.

The Bible is essential to us, and a necessary guide to help us win this race which is our life here on earth. St Augustine, Bishop of Hippo once said: *"The God who created you can not save you without you"* St Augustine, Sermo 169,13 (PL38,923). Meanwhile this same God who cannot save us without our cooperation has ensured to give us all the help we need in addition to paying the price to save us by offering Jesus, His only son for our sake.

The Bible is for our own good!

PRAYER

Loving Father, You created me for a purpose and return to You at the end of my days, if I will live in a way that is pleasing to You, and You made Your Word to guide me for this. Please give me the grace to meditate on it, the mind to understand it and the disposition to do Your Will and be with You at the end of my race, in Jesus' Name. Amen.

ABOUT THE AUTHOR

Of dual heritage, passionate about her faith, this mother of four had her first encounter at the tender age of 4.

She pioneered a children & young people's group in her Community "the Friends of Jesus" and engaged in various program deliveries such as talks, catechism lesson, and sponsored charitable organisations.

Ardent in her belief, she has on this occasion transferred the practice of her faith into this book as a way of sharing and fundraising, giving part of the proceeds of sale from this book to charitable organisations.

Printed in Great Britain
by Amazon

87539213R00068